THE LITTLE GOLF POETRY BOOK

WALTER THE EDUCATOR

THE LITTLE GOLF POETRY BOOK

SKB

Silent King Books a WhichHead Entertainment Imprint

Disclaimer
This book is a literary work; poems are not about specific persons, locations, situations, and/or circumstances unless mentioned in historical context. This book is for entertainment and informational purposes only. The author and publisher offer this information without warranties expressed or implied. No matter the grounds, neither the author nor the publisher will be accountable for any losses, injuries, or other damages caused by the reader's use of this book. The use of this book acknowledges an understanding and acceptance of this disclaimer.

dedicated to all the golf lovers in the world

CONTENTS

CONTENTS

CONTENTS

CONTENTS

CONTENTS

WHY I CREATED A GOLF POETRY BOOK?

Known for being one of the world's most popular sport, The Little Golf Poetry Book includes unique poems representing Golf topics associated with the lovable game, making it the perfect gift for the Golf lover. Creating a poetry book about Golf can be a unique way of exploring the game. Poetry can give a fresh perspective and bring an imaginative approach to understanding and appreciating the game of Golf. Moreover, it can bridge the gap between sports and art and appeal to a larger audience. Overall, a poetry book about Golf can be an appealing and creative way to engage with the game that so many people love.

CHAPTER

ONE

A GLORIOUS DREAM

Golf is a game of patience and skill,
Where the greens and fairways meet the hills.
The swing of the club, the sound of the ball,
A moment of focus, before it takes flight and falls.

The sun beats down, the breeze is light,
Golfers seek the perfect sight.
The ball is hit, it soars with grace,
Towards the hole, a hopeful race.

The course ahead, a challenge to face,
A test of strength, precision, and pace.
The sand traps, the rough, the water's edge,
Obstacles to overcome, to reach the final pledge.

The joy of success, the frustration of defeat,
Golfers strive to improve their feat.

The camaraderie, the beauty of the scene,
A game of golf, a glorious dream.
    So let us play, with heart and soul,
And strive to reach our ultimate goal.
For in the game of golf, we find,
A challenge that enriches the mind.

PRECISION AND SKILL

Golf is a game of precision and skill,
Of greens and fairways, and putters that thrill.
A ball that's small, yet travels so far,
Through sand traps and rough, and water that's hard.
The swing of a club, a perfect arc,
The ball takes flight, like a soaring lark.
The sound of the shot, a satisfying ping,
A hole in one, the ultimate win.
The course is vast, a beauty to behold,
A challenge to conquer, a story to be told.
The sun beats down, the wind howls strong,
Yet the golfers march on, with a determined song.
Golf is more than just a game,
It's a test of character, and a chance for fame.

The camaraderie that comes with golf,
Is what makes this game a treasure trove.
    So let's play a round, and enjoy the breeze,
As we swing our clubs with ease.
For in this game, we find peace and fun,
And the memories we make, will last a lifetime, long.

CHAPTER

FOUR

WE GIVE IT OUR ALL

Golf is a game of patience and skill
Played with joy and pride, the heart to fill
The greens and fairways stretch so wide
Challenges abound, but we take them in stride
    The swing, the putt, the perfect shot
The ball takes flight, oh what a thought
The wind may blow, the rain may fall
But we play on, we give it our all
    The sand traps and water hazards too
Can make us stumble, but we push through
We learn from each game, each mistake
And strive to improve, for the love of the game's sake
    The camaraderie, the memories we make
Are just as important, make no mistake

We bond with friends, both old and new
And cherish the moments, the laughter and hue
    Golf is more than just a game
It's a challenge, a joy, a passion aflame
It teaches us patience, discipline, and grace
And leaves us with memories, that time cannot erase.

CHAPTER

FIVE

BEAUTY TO BEHOLD

Golf, a game of precision and skill,
A challenge to conquer, a test of will.
The greens and fairways, so pristine,
A beauty to behold, like a dream.

The obstacles lie ahead, the bunkers and trees,
A puzzle to solve, if you aim to please.
The sand traps and water hazards too,
A golfer's nightmare, but a challenge anew.

The swing of the club, the ball in flight,
A moment of truth, a pure delight.
The birdies and eagles, the cheers and applause,
A golfer's dream, a moment to pause.

A lifelong passion, a love affair,
The game of golf, beyond compare.

A sport of kings, a game for all,
A journey of a lifetime, a thrill to recall.

GOLF COURSE GOLD

The green stretches out before my feet,
A sea of grass, so lush and neat.
The sun shines down, a warm embrace,
As I prepare to swing with grace.

The ball soars high, against the blue,
A sight so pure, a dream come true.
The wind whispers softly in my ear,
Guiding the ball, so it may steer.

With each shot, I feel alive,
A sense of purpose, I cannot deny.
The fairways lead me on my way,
A journey I cherish, day by day.

The bunkers, the trees, the water so clear,
Each obstacle, I must conquer, without fear.

The challenge is great, but so is the reward,
For every hole, a chance to score.
     At the end of the day, as the sun sets low,
I look back, on the course, all aglow.
The memories, the moments, the friendships made,
A treasure of gold, that will never fade.

ROLLING HILLS

Golfing greens and rolling hills,
A challenge for the heart and wills,
The wind may blow, the sand may shift,
But nothing stops the golfer's gift.

The fairway stretches far and wide,
A test of skill, a test of pride,
The golfer's swing, a graceful art,
Aiming true with every part.

The ball takes flight, across the green,
A distant target, yet unseen,
The golfer's eye, a keen insight,
Aiming true with all their might.

The green awaits, a gentle slope,
A careful putt, a prayer and hope,

The ball rolls true, the cup in sight,
A perfect end to a perfect flight.
    The game of golf, a noble quest,
A challenge for the very best,
The golfer's heart, a steady beat,
A passion that can never be beat.

FINESSE

Golf is a game of finesse and skill,
A challenge to conquer with every thrill.
The course is a canvas, green and vast,
A place where players' abilities are cast.

The fairways stretch out, a path to follow,
With bunkers and hazards, a test to swallow.
The greens are the prize, a target to hit,
A challenge that requires both power and wit.

Each hole is unique, a puzzle to solve,
A task that requires patience and resolve.
The wind is a factor, a force to contend,
A factor that can make or break a trend.

But despite the challenges, golf is a delight,
A game that rewards both effort and sight.

The beauty of the course, the camaraderie too,
Make golf a game that is forever true.
    So swing with grace, putt with care,
And enjoy the game that is beyond compare.
For golf is not just a game, but a way of life,
A journey of self-discovery, amidst the strife.

HIS DREAMS TO KEEP

On the green grass of the golf course,
The golfer stands with poise and force.
The club in hand, the ball in sight,
He swings with all his strength and might.

The ball takes flight, soaring high,
Against the blue and cloudless sky.
It lands with grace, a gentle thud,
As the golfer's heart fills with blood.

He walks the course, with care and skill,
Avoiding hazards, with nerves of steel.
The wind may blow, the sun may shine,
But the golfer's focus is always fine.

The course is vast, with hills and bends,
But the golfer knows each twist and trend.

He navigates the fairways with ease,
His passion for golf, forever to please.
    The game of golf, a challenge and delight,
A test of skill, with every stroke in sight.
The golfer's heart, with passion deep,
Forever on the course, his dreams to keep.

PURE DELIGHT

Golf is a game of finesse and skill,
Where the course is a canvas, players fill.
Each hole a unique puzzle to solve,
Patience and resolve required to evolve.
The greens a lush carpet of green,
The fairways a sight to be seen.
Bunkers and hazards, a challenge to face,
Yet the rewards make the journey worth the race.
Golf is not just a game, but a way of life,
A journey of self-discovery, free from strife.
The wind, the sun, the rain, all part of the game,
The joy of playing, always the same.
The golf course a place of beauty and grace,
A sanctuary to find one's pace.

An escape from the noise of modern days,
A chance to reconnect in so many ways.
   So let us tee off and take to the course,
And let our spirits take flight like a horse.
For golf is a game that rewards effort and sight,
And fills our hearts with pure delight.

A TALE OF GREENS AND FAIRWAYS

In fields of green and sunlit skies,
Where ancient hills and valleys rise,
A game was born, so pure and true,
To test the heart and skill of few.
The Scots, they say, were first to play,
On misty dawns and windy days,
With clubs of wood and balls of lead,
They forged a sport that would be read.
The links of St. Andrews, how they shone,
A mecca for the game, a home,
Where legends like Old Tom and Young,
Would rule the roost and sing their song.
From Scotland's shores, the game did spread,

To England, Ireland, and beyond we read,
To colonies and lands afar,
Where fairways stretched and courses par.

From hickory sticks to modern gear,
The game endured, year after year,
With tales of triumph, heartbreak, lore,
And legends that we still adore.

So, let us toast this game of kings,
Of birdies, bogeys, eagles, swings,
Where skill and patience, wit and charm,
Combine to make a round so warm.

For golf is more than just a game,
It's a journey, a test, a claim,
To be the best, to reach the top,
To never stop, to never drop.

And so, we tee it up and go,
With hopes and dreams, with highs and lows,
To chase the ball, to chase the dream,
To play the game, and hear it scream.

EVOLVED AND CHANGE

Golf, a sport of precision and grace
Played on green fields and open space
Its roots can be traced to ancient time
When Romans played a game called Paganica, sublime
But it was Scotland that gave birth
To the modern game we know and cherish on earth
In the 15th century, the Scots played a game
Called "gowf" that was a precursor to the fame
The first golf course was built in St. Andrews
And soon, the game spread like wildfire and embers
It became a sport of kings and nobility
Played with clubs and balls of varying ability
Over time, the game evolved and changed
New rules and techniques were exchanged

From wooden clubs to modern-day drivers
Golf has stood the test of time and survived us
    Today, golf is enjoyed by millions worldwide
From amateurs to pros who take pride
In mastering the art of the game
And leaving their mark on golf's hall of fame
    So, let's raise a glass to golf's history
And the joys it brings to us in all its glory
May it continue to be a beloved sport
That we can all play and enjoy, in every sort.

GOLF ENDURES

From Scotland's rolling hills,
A game was born, so pure and still.
With clubs and balls, and endless greens,
A sport was born, for kings and queens.
    The Scots played first, with skill and grace,
And soon the game spread to every place.
From England's links to America's shores,
Golf became the game that everyone adores.
    The fairways stretched for miles and miles,
And every golfer wore a smile.
The bunkers posed a challenge true,
But golfers knew just what to do.
The putter in hand, the ball in sight,
The golfer aimed with all their might.

A tap, a roll, and in it went,
The crowd erupted, wild and spent.
    For golf is more than just a game,
It's a way of life, a passion flame.
It tests your skill, your mind, your heart,
And every round, a brand new start.
    So let us celebrate this sport,
This game of greens and fairways wrought.
From ancient times to modern days,
Golf endures, in every way.

THE GAME OF LEGENDS

On green fields and rolling hills,
The game of golf, a story spills.
From ancient lands and Scottish hills,
Legends of golf, the air stills.
In days of old, it's said with pride,
Shepherds used their crooks to guide
Small balls into rabbit holes,
A pastime that would soon unfold.
Mary Queen of Scots, the story goes,
Played golf with clubs and balls she chose.
And from that day, the game took hold,
In every corner, stories told.
From St. Andrews to Augusta's course,
Golf is played with passion and force.

The legends of the game still thrive,
As golfers strive to stay alive.
From Bobby Jones to Tiger Woods,
They've won the game with skill and goods.
Legends of golf, forever etched,
Their stories, never to be fetched.
On green fields and rolling hills,
The game of golf, a story spills.
From ancient lands and Scottish hills,
Legends of golf, the air stills.

RICH IN LORE

The game of golf, so rich in lore,
Originated on Scotland's shore.
In fields and hills, the Scotsmen played,
Hitting balls with clubs, their skills displayed.

The first recorded game, they say,
Was played in Fifeshire one fine day.
A ball was struck with wooden stick,
And so began a game so slick.

The legends of the game abound,
From Bobby Jones to Tiger's sound.
Arnold Palmer, Nicklaus too,
Their skills and talents, we all knew.

The Masters, Open, PGA,
The tournaments we watch each day.

The skill and grace of every stroke,
The legends of the game, bespoke.
    The game of golf, a sport so grand,
Played on courses throughout the land.
A game of skill, precision, and grace,
A legendary sport for every race.

SPIRIT OF THE GAME

Golf, a game of skill and grace,
Played on greens where golfers race,
To hit a ball with clubs so fine,
And send it soaring down the line.

Originating in ancient times,
From shepherds who hit rocks with chimes,
To pass the time while tending flocks,
And test their strength upon the rocks.

But now, with courses lush and grand,
Golfers roam across the land,
To play the game with style and poise,
And hear the roar of crowds' applause.

The swing, the putt, and all the rest,
Are tests of skill at their very best,

And players strive to be the one,
To sink the ball and claim the fun.
    So let us honor this great game,
And all its players, known by name,
For they have shown us how to strive,
And keep the spirit of the game alive.

MAGIC THAT GOLF BRINGS

Golf, a game of skill and grace,
Played on greens with clubs in place.
A sport that's steeped in history,
With mysteries wrapped in mystery.

Its origin shrouded in the past,
As players hit balls with a cast.
Some say it's from Scotland's coast,
Where links were found by those engrossed.

The rules have changed throughout the years,
From handicap to strokes and tiers.
But one thing remains the same,
The thrill of victory, the joy of the game.

Now players tee off with a smile,
Driving balls for mile after mile.

They putt and chip with finesse,
And hope for par or nothing less.
    So if you're looking for a game,
With challenges that will put you to shame,
Grab your clubs and hit the links,
And discover the magic that golf brings.

SERENE AND CALM

The game of Golf, so serene and calm,
A sport that requires skill and aplomb.
Its origin shrouded in mystery and lore,
But its history we honor and adore.
From Scottish fields to modern greens,
The game has evolved through many scenes.
With clubs and balls, we take our aim,
And strive for glory, fortune, and fame.
The swing of the club and the ball's flight,
Are a testament to skill and might.
The precision and focus required to play,
Are what make Golf a sport of the highest sway.
With every shot, we learn and grow,
And the love of the game continues to flow.

We honor the players and their dedication,
To keeping the spirit of Golf alive with passion.
    So let us tee off and begin the game,
With a heart full of joy and a spirit untamed.
For in Golf, we find a beauty that endures,
A game that teaches and inspires, and forever assures.

HONOR AND GRACE

Golf, a game of skill and grace,
Played on greens, a peaceful place.
Steeped in history, shrouded in mystery,
Its origin, a tale of victory.

From Scotland, the game did spread,
To England, America, and beyond it led.
The rules have changed throughout the years,
But the joy of the game still brings cheers.

A challenge of precision and control,
A test of patience, body, and soul.
From the tee to the hole, each shot counts,
A game of strategy, no lucky amounts.

The sound of the club, the ball in flight,
The beauty of the course, a breathtaking sight.

The thrill of victory, the agony of defeat,
Yet the love of the game cannot be beat.
So grab your clubs and hit the links,
Discover the magic that golf brings.
A game of tradition, honor, and grace,
Golf, a sport that time cannot erase.

A TRUE LEGACY

Golf, a game of skill and grace,
Originating in Scotland's green space,
Where men would hit a ball with a stick,
And chase it down with a competitive flick.

The rules were simple, yet refined,
To strike the ball and keep in mind,
To get it in the hole with fewest shots,
And avoid the hazards, like bunkers and pots.

The courses were vast and beautifully made,
With rolling hills and trees that swayed,
A true test of one's mental and physical might,
To conquer the game and play it right.

Golf has evolved and grown in time,
With new rules and gear that shine,

But at its core, it remains the same,
A game of patience, strategy, and aim.
  So let's grab our clubs and hit the links,
And sink that ball with a confident wink,
For golf is more than a game, you see,
It's a way of life, a true legacy.

TEST OF SKILL

Golf, a game of precision and grace,
A sport that stands in a class of its own race,
With origins that date back to ancient times,
When shepherds played with sticks and stones.
   The rules and regulations have evolved with time,
From the number of holes to the length of the line,
From the proper etiquette to the dress code,
Golfers must follow them, as they hit the road.
   The greens are lush, the fairways pristine,
The bunkers, the water hazards, make the game keen,
The swing, the putt, the chip, and the drive,
All come together to make the game thrive.
   Golf is a game of mental might,
To conquer the course, one must have the insight,

To read the wind, the slope, and the lie,
And with a steady hand, make the ball fly.
 So, take up your club, and hit the links,
Play with passion, and let your heart sing,
For the game of golf is a beautiful thing,
A true test of skill, a joy to bring.

SKIES ABOVE

In the fields of Scotland, long ago,
A game was born, that we all know,
With clubs and balls, and a simple goal,
To hit the ball, and make it roll.
The game of golf, it quickly spread,
With players flocking to the green and the red,
To play the links, and test their skill,
And find out who had the strongest will.
But how did they play, in those early days,
Without the swing, that we all praise,
They simply hit, with a simple stroke,
And hoped the ball, would not provoke.
It was a man named Willie Park,
Who first developed, the modern arc,

With a swing so smooth, so fluid, so fine,
It changed the game, for all of time.
    Now we all swing, with power and grace,
And try to win, the elusive race,
To be the best, on the course of green,
And show the world, what we can glean.
    So let us honor, the game we love,
And the swing that came, from the skies above,
And play with passion, and play with heart,
And let our swings, set us apart.

SLOW AND STEADY

Golf, a game of skill and grace,
A sport that takes you to a peaceful place.
The origin of this game is hard to trace,
But the golf swing is one that we all embrace.

From the Scottish hills, it made its way,
Across the oceans, it came to stay.
The golf swing, a thing of beauty,
A motion that's both strong and fruity.

It starts with a stance, feet shoulder-width apart,
Eyes on the ball, with a focus on the heart.
The backswing, slow and steady,
With arms and club, both held ready.

At the top, a brief pause,
Before the downswing, which is the cause.

The hips, they turn, the arms follow through,
The ball takes flight, as if on cue.

The sound of the club, as it meets the ball,
Is music to the ears, a sweet siren's call.

Golf, a game of patience and pride,
A sport that's cherished far and wide.

With the golf swing, we seek perfection,
A timeless quest, a golfer's obsession.

A FLUID MOTION

In Scotland's rolling hills,
A game was born with clubs and balls.
Golf, it was called, a test of skill,
To hit a target, conquer its sprawl.

The swing was crude, a mighty heave,
With wooden clubs and leather gloves.
But soon a man named Willie Park,
Changed the game with his gentle arc.

A fluid motion, a graceful dance,
The modern swing was born that day.
With passion, heart, and a little chance,
Golfers took to the course to play.

Now golf is played across the land,
In courses grand and small.

The game is steeped in tradition,
And honors those who play with gall.
So swing your club with purpose true,
And let your heart guide every shot.
For golf is more than just a game,
It's a journey, a passion, a lot.

THE STANCE

In Scotland's rolling hills and greens,
A sport was born, or so it seems,
A game of skill, of strength, of grace,
That challenges the human race.

The golf swing, a thing of beauty,
A fluid motion, a golfer's duty,
To strike the ball with perfect aim,
And watch it soar, without shame.

The stance, a crucial part of play,
Feet apart, arms straight, we sway,
And with a mighty swing of might,
We send the ball into flight.

From humble beginnings, golf did rise,
To capture hearts, and challenge eyes,

A game of honor, and fair play,
That's why we love it, to this day.
  So grab your clubs, and hit the course,
Let's play the game, with no remorse,
For in this game, we find our peace,
And let our worries, slowly cease.

A SOARING SPARK

From Scotland's rolling hills it came
A game of skill, of grace, of aim
A pastime for the wealthy few
Now enjoyed by many, me and you
　The golf swing, a marvel to behold
A motion graceful, yet so bold
A twisting turn, a fluid arc
The ball takes flight, a soaring spark
　The stance, a foundation strong and sure
Feet planted firm, a posture pure
The grip, a subtle art in play
A steady hand, to guide the way
　From tee to green, the journey long
With hazards lurking, waiting strong

The golfer, a master of his craft,
Navigating the course, with each shot, a draft.
   The game of golf, a test of patience and will,
A journey of self-discovery, a thrill,
The origins of the golf swing, a legacy to behold,
A game of tradition, forever to unfold.

SO SMOOTH AND TRUE

Golf, a game that's played with grace
With clubs in hand, we take our place
A sport that's ancient, yet still we play
On greens that stretch for miles away
From Scotland's hills, it first did come
A game for all, not just for some
With wooden clubs and feathered balls
They'd play for hours, till night would fall
And then came the swing, so smooth and true
A motion that we still pursue
A backswing slow, then down it goes
The ball takes flight, as everyone knows
The putter too, a stroke of skill
To roll it straight, with just a little thrill

The ball it rolls, so slow and true
And drops into the cup, like morning dew
    So let us play, this game of old
With clubs in hand, and hearts so bold
For on the greens, we find our peace
And let life's troubles, finally cease.

SINKING THE PERFECT PUT

Golf, a game of precision and skill,
Where players swing and hit with will.
The ball soars high in the sky,
As players strive to hit it just right.

But how did this game come to be?
Let me tell you a story, just you and me.
In ancient times, in Scotland's green,
Shepherds would use their crooks to hit pebbles keen.

As time passed by, the game evolved,
And people started to get involved.
They used clubs made of wood and iron,
And the game spread far and wide like a lion.

And then came the putting, the art so fine,
Where players aim the ball to the tiny line.

With a gentle stroke and a steady hand,
They guide the ball to the promised land.
    So next time you hit the links,
Remember the game's origin and its important links.
And when you sink that perfect putt,
You'll feel the joy, the thrill, the rush.

PUTTING GREEN

Golf, the sport of kings,
Where men and women swing,
With clubs and balls in hand,
To conquer the greens and sand.

Born in Scotland's rolling hills,
Where sheep roamed and streams still,
Golf was played with sticks and stones,
By shepherds with hearts of gold.

Now it's a game of fame and skill,
Played by pros with nerves of steel,
Who conquer the greens and holes,
With precision and control.

Putting is the ultimate test,
Where the ball must roll to rest,

In the hole just a few feet away,
To win the game and save the day.
    Golf is a journey of joy and pain,
Of challenges and triumphs gained,
Where the journey is the reward,
And the putting green the final chord.

CHAPTER

THIRTY-ONE

VICTORY IS SWEET

The green stretches out before me,
A challenge I must face,
With club in hand, I take my stance,
And set my eyes on the space.

A gentle breeze, a whispered hush,
As I begin my stroke,
The ball rolls true, towards the hole,
My heart begins to hope.

The crowd holds its breath,
As the ball draws near,
Will it drop in the cup,
Or will it veer?

But I am focused, steady,
My aim is true and pure,

And with a satisfying click,
The ball falls in for sure.
    Victory is sweet,
As I walk off the green,
A triumphant smile on my face,
At this game of golf, serene.

THE SCORECARD
NEVER LIES

On the green, the ball rolls true
A gentle tap, a perfect view
The scorecard waits, ready to fill
Each stroke a story, each hole a thrill
    The handicap, a fairer chance
To level the field, to enhance
The challenge of this ancient game
Where every shot can bring fame
    The wind may blow, the sun may shine
But the scorecard never lies
It's a test of nerve, of strategy too
And a chance to see what you can do
    So let the clubs do the talking

As you walk the fairways, never stopping
For in this game of golf and scoring
The journey is always worth exploring.

THE FAIRWAYS WIDE

Golf, a game of patience and tact,
A battle played on grassy tract.
With clubs in hand and ball in sight,
The golfer's goal is clear and bright.

The scorecard waits, a challenge set,
Each stroke a chance to gain or fret.
The handicap, a foe to beat,
A test of skill, both strong and fleet.

The fairways wide, the greens so true,
The challenge great for me and you.
The flagstick waves, a beacon bright,
A target set, a goal in sight.

So swing away, with grace and ease,
And watch the ball take flight with these.

For golf is more than just a game,
It's skill and heart, a quest for fame.
    And when the round is done and through,
The scores are tallied, dreams come true.
For in this game of skill and will,
The test is won by those with thrill.

GREEN AND BLUE

Golf, a sport of green and blue,
Where skies meet grass, and dreams come true.
The thrill of the swing, the crack of the ball,
The journey of the game, where we give it our all.

Handicapping, a fair challenge in play,
Leveling the field, day by day.
Scores may differ, but the spirit remains,
As we strive for improvement, despite any pains.

The course, a canvas, where we paint our game,
A canvas that changes, never quite the same.
Each stroke a challenge, each hole a test,
As we aim for the flag, and strive for our best.

So let us embrace this game of golf,
With all its challenges, be it easy or tough.

For the score is just a number, in the end,
It's the journey we take, that helps us transcend.

A GAME FOR ALL

Golf, a sport of green and blue,
Where the grass is trimmed like new,
A place where people come to play,
And spend their leisure hours away.
The swing of the club, the hit of the ball,
The sound of it soaring, over the wall,
The cheers of the crowd, the thrill of the game,
Golf is more than just a sport, it's a fame.
From small towns to big cities,
Everyone's a fan, no matter their identities,
Golf is a game for all,
Young and old, big and small.
The popularity of golf is not a mystery,
It's the beauty of the course, the history,

The challenge of the game, the camaraderie,
That makes it an enduring legacy.
    So come, swing your club, hit the ball,
Feel the excitement, have a ball,
Golf is more than just a game,
It's a passion, a love, a fame.

ARTFUL SWAY

Golf, a sport of artful sway,
Where swings and putts are made to play,
With every stroke, the grasses sway,
And golfers watch their balls take flight.

The tees, the greens, the bunkers deep,
All challenges to make us weep,
But true golfers take it in stride,
And with every shot, they take in pride.

The wind may blow, the sun may shine,
But golfers know it's all divine,
For in this game, they find their peace,
And with each shot, their joy increases.

So let us raise our clubs up high,
And watch our balls against the sky,

For in this game, we find our thrill,
And with each round, our hearts are filled.

SPORT SO SERENE

Golf, a sport so serene,
Where the grass is always green,
And the wind whispers in your ear,
As you line up your shot without fear.

The swing of the club, so smooth and light,
Brings a sense of joy, so pure and bright,
As the ball soars through the air,
You can't help but stop and stare.

With each shot, comes a new challenge,
But never once does it feel like a scrimmage,
For the love of the game is strong,
And in your heart, it will forever belong.

The greens are like a canvas, so vast,
And with each stroke, you create a masterpiece that

will last,
A work of art that's unique to you,
And in that moment, there's nothing else you need
to do.
    So here's to the game that we all adore,
Where the challenges are aplenty, but never a bore,
For in the end, it's the journey that counts,
And the memories we make on every single ounce.

THE FAIRWAY CALLS

Golf, a sport of artful sway,
Where players take pride in every play,
Each stroke a canvas, a work of art,
A masterpiece created from the heart.
The fairway calls, the green awaits,
The challenge of the game, we savor and celebrate,
Each hole a journey, a unique test,
And with each shot, we give our best.
The sound of the club, the rush of the swing,
The ball takes flight, a beautiful thing,
The wind whispers secrets, the sun smiles bright,
And with every shot, we find our delight.
Golf is more than just a game,
It's a passion, a joy, a thrill to claim,

A way of life, a source of peace,
Where we find release from the daily grind's disease.
   So let us take to the course with pride,
And let our love for golf never subside,
For in this game, we find our bliss,
And nothing can ever top a round of this.

FOR GOLF IS MY LOVE

Golf is a game like no other,
A passion that I cannot smother.
From the club in my hand,
To the ball on the stand,
I feel my heart begin to flutter.
Each swing is like a work of art,
A dance with the club, I take part.
The ball flies through the air,
With grace and with flair,
And I feel a flutter in my heart.
The green is my sanctuary,
A place where I can be merry.
The wind in my hair,

The sun on my skin fair,
And my heart beats like a canary.
    Golf is a game that I adore,
A love that I cannot ignore.
With every stroke and putt,
I feel like I'm in a rut,
Until I hear the sound of the score.
    So I'll keep on playing this game,
And let my heart be aflame.
For golf is my love,
A gift from above,
And I'll never be the same.

LOVE AFFAIR

On the green, I feel at peace,
My only worries are the clubs I lease.
A love affair, that's what it is,
My heart beats fast with every swing and miss.
The fairway stretches, inviting me in,
With each shot, I feel like I could win.
The wind whispers secrets in my ear,
As I line up my ball, without any fear.
The hole, my ultimate goal,
With each stroke, I feel whole.
The sound of the ball, as it drops in,
Is sweeter than any love I've ever been in.
Golf, my passion, my heart and soul,
Will always be the love that makes me whole.

Walter the Educator is one of the pseudonyms for Walter Anderson. Formally educated in Chemistry, Business, and Education, he is an educator, an author, a diverse entrepreneur, and the son of a disabled war veteran. "Walter the Educator" shares his time between educating and creating. He holds interests and owns several creative projects that entertain, enlighten, enhance, and educate, hoping to inspire and motivate you.

Follow, find new works, and stay up to date with Walter the Educator at

www.WaltertheEducator.com

Printed in the USA
CPSIA information can be obtained
at www.ICGtesting.com
LVHW021644191223
766915LV00014B/500